Mandala

MAGIC

COLORING BOOK

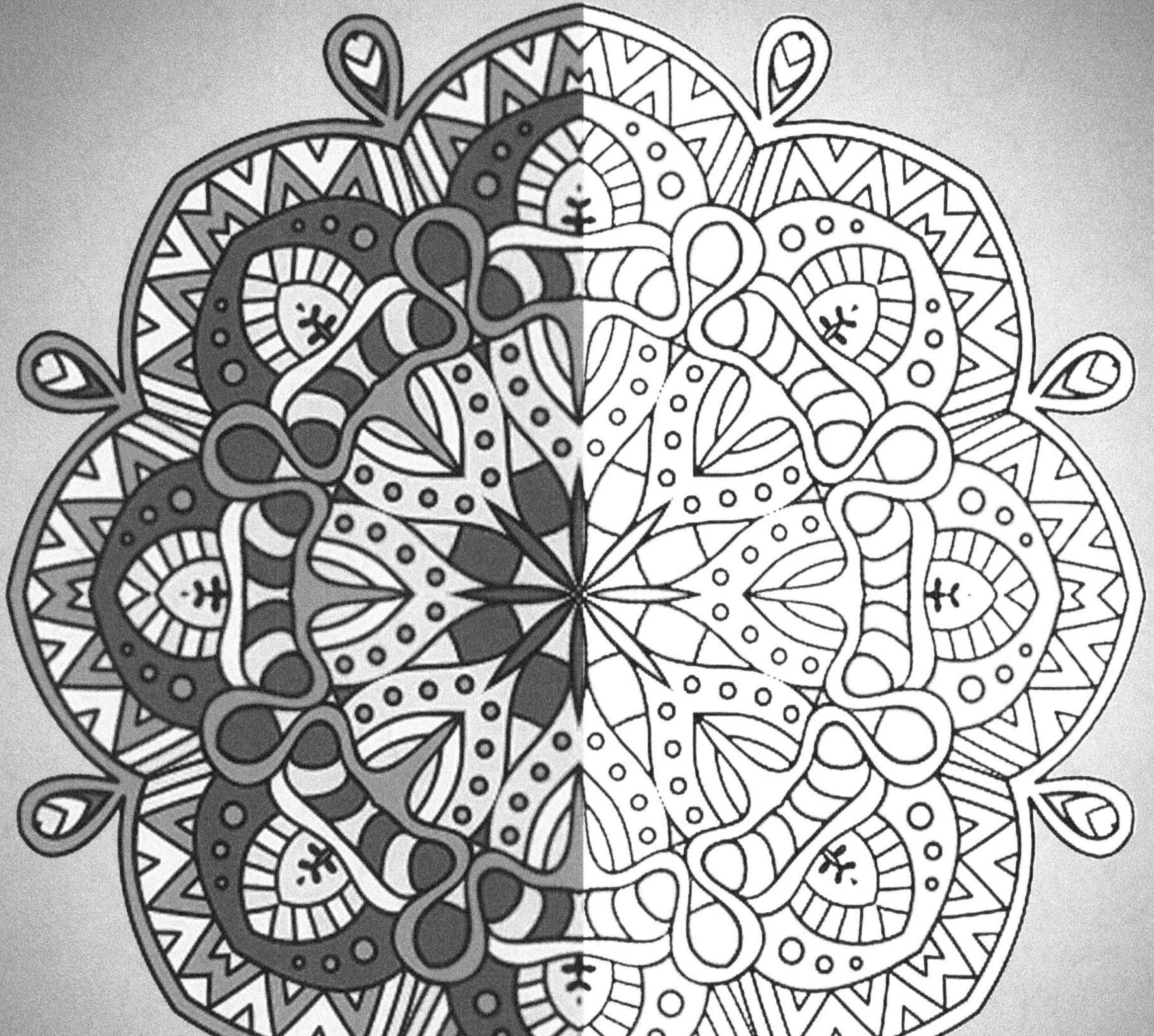

COLOR TEST PAGE

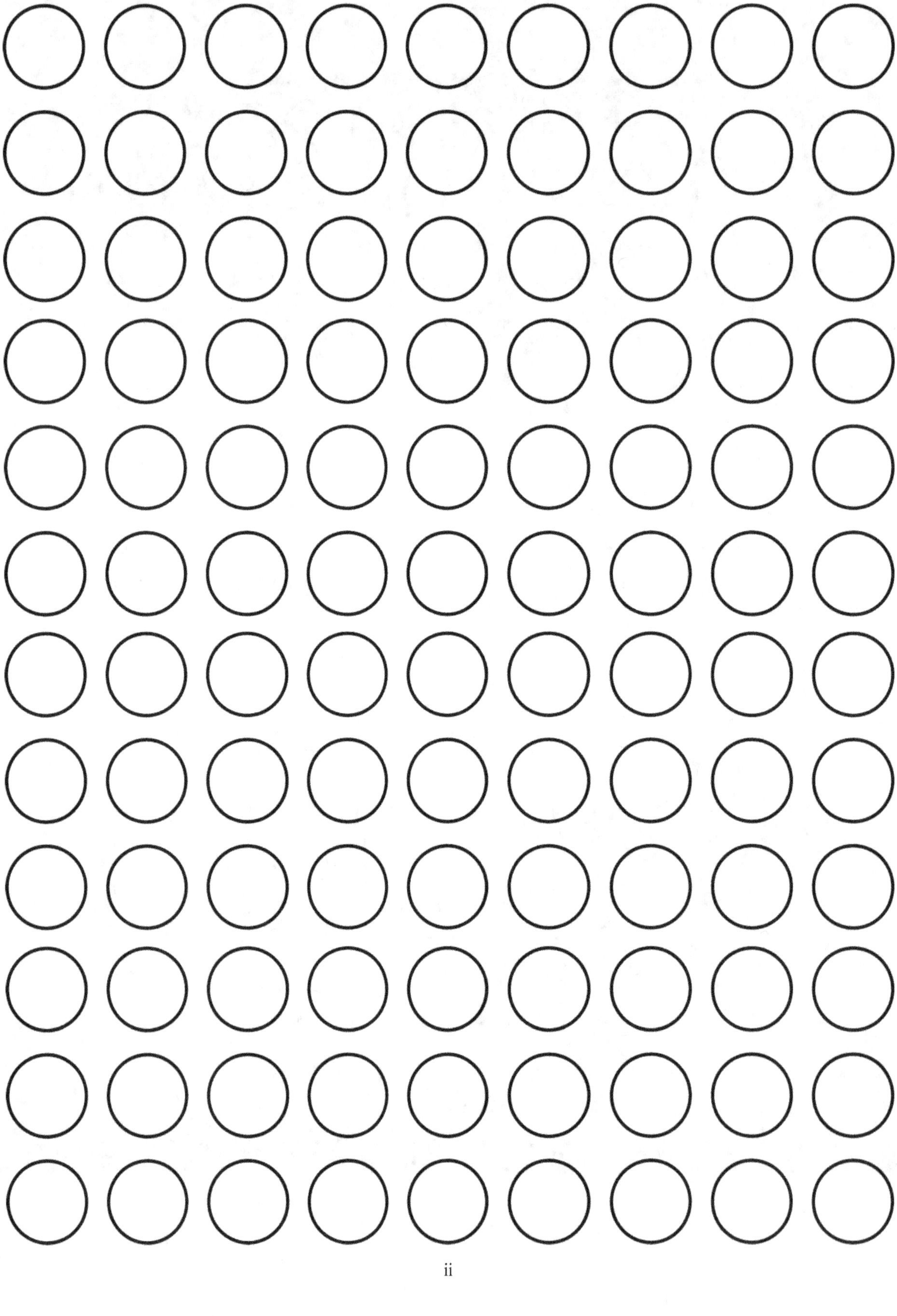

COLOR TEST PAGE

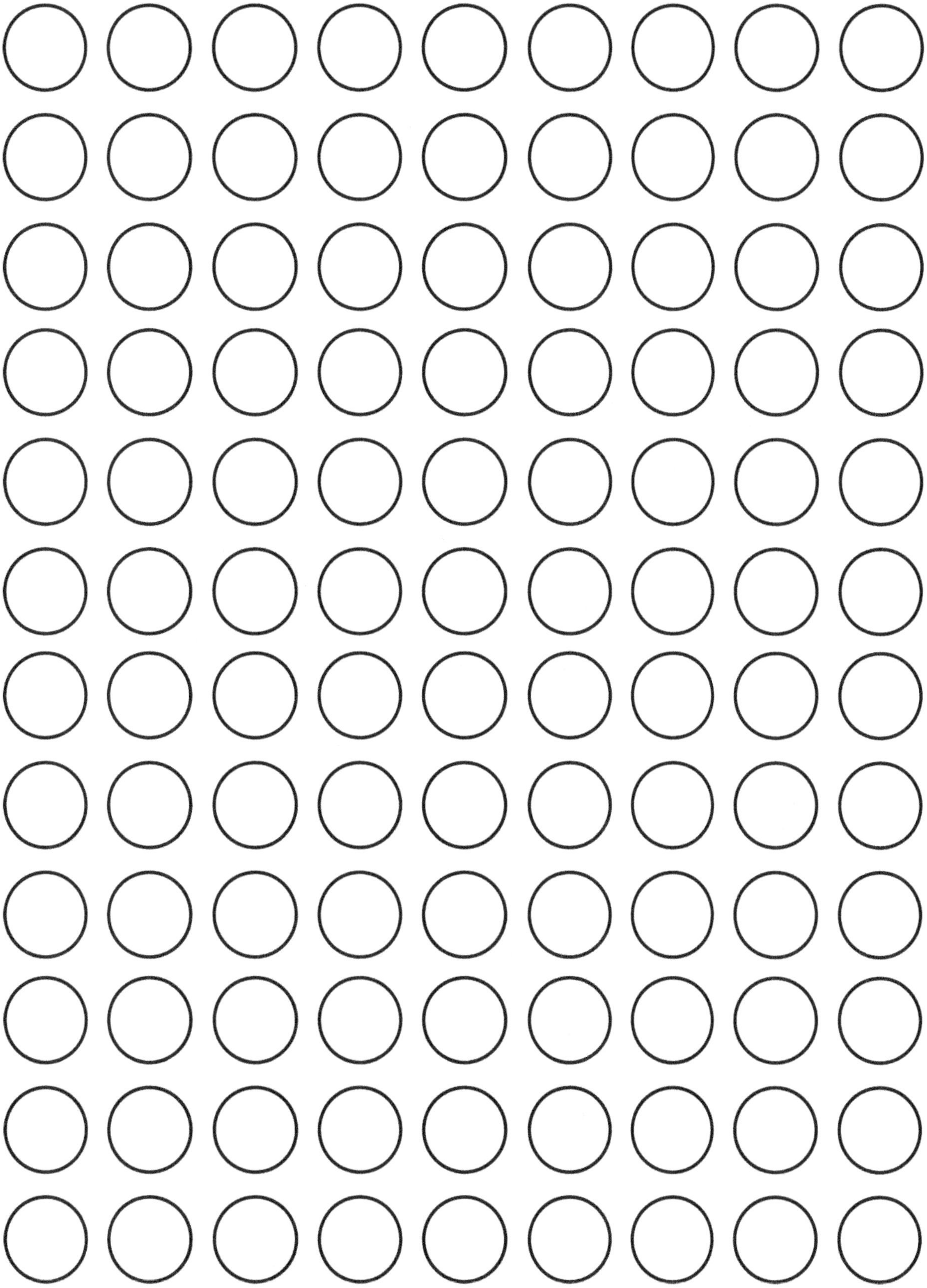

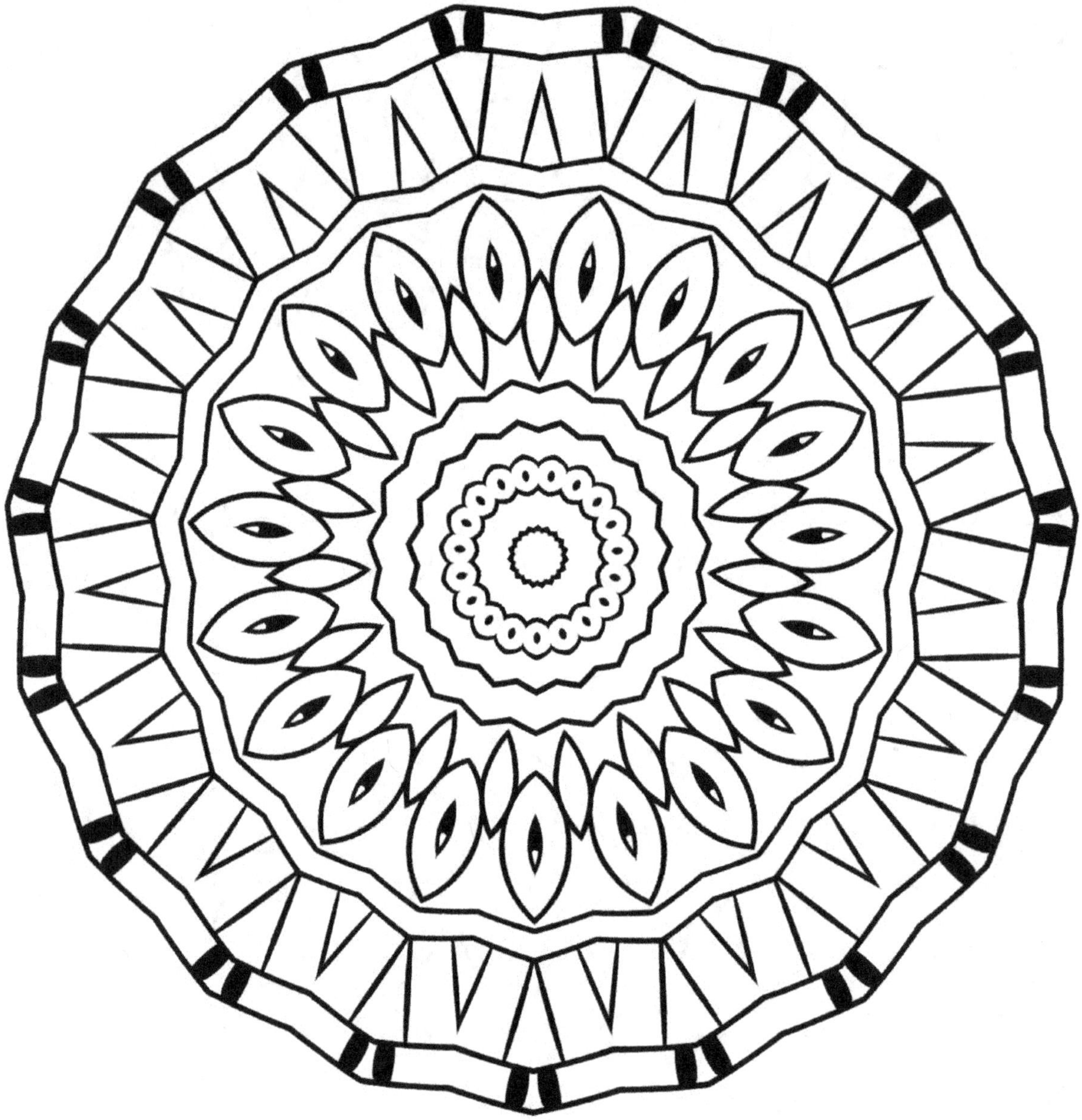

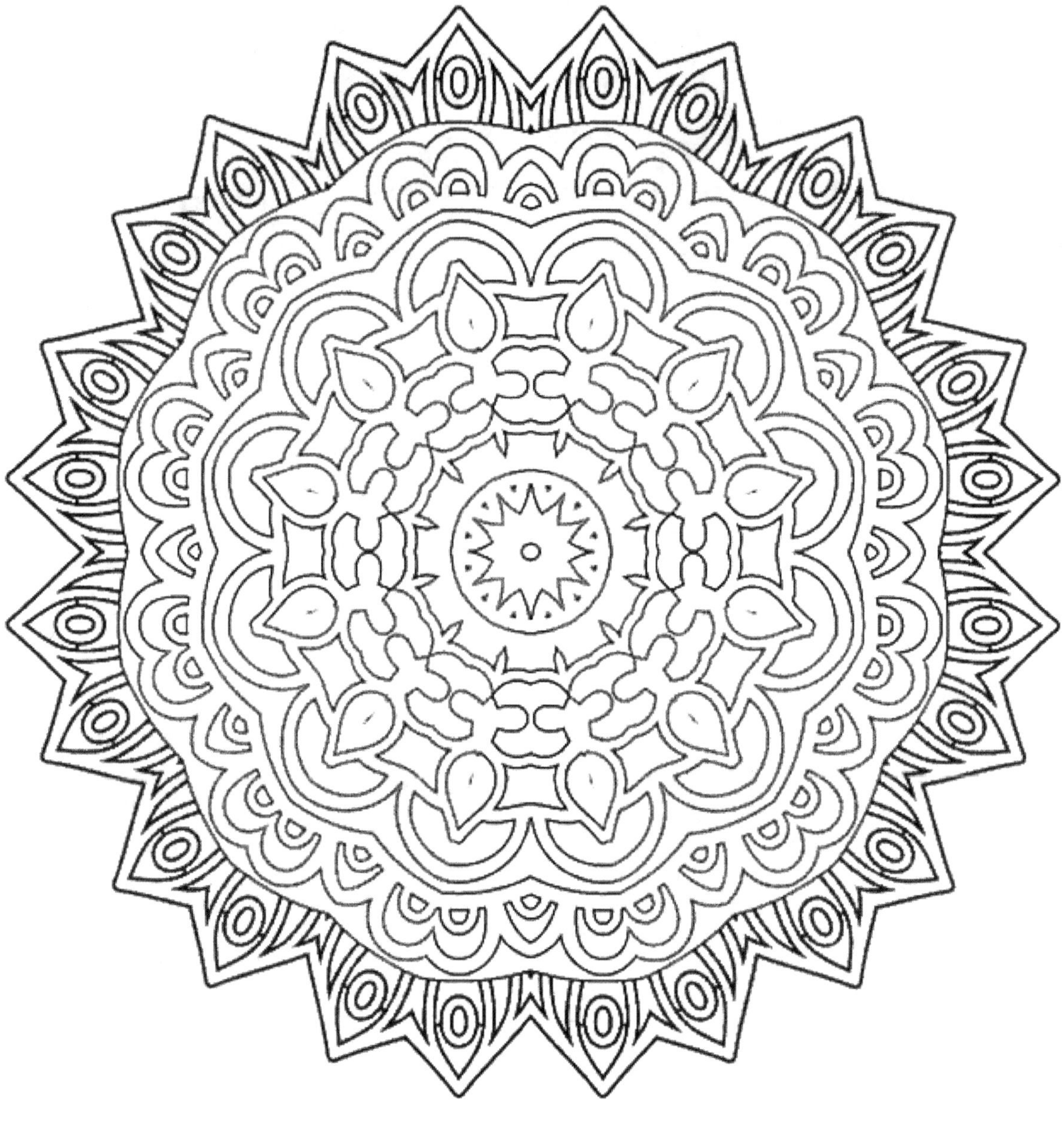

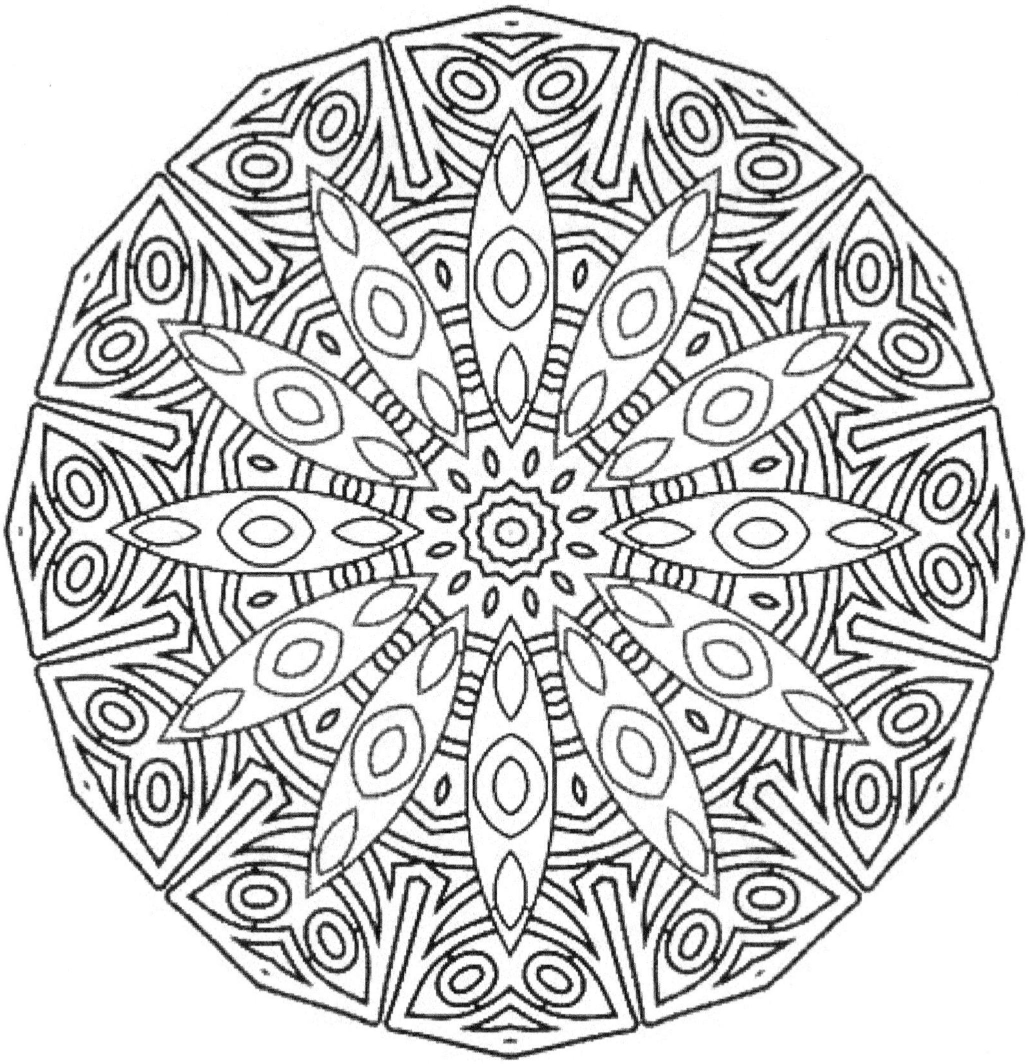

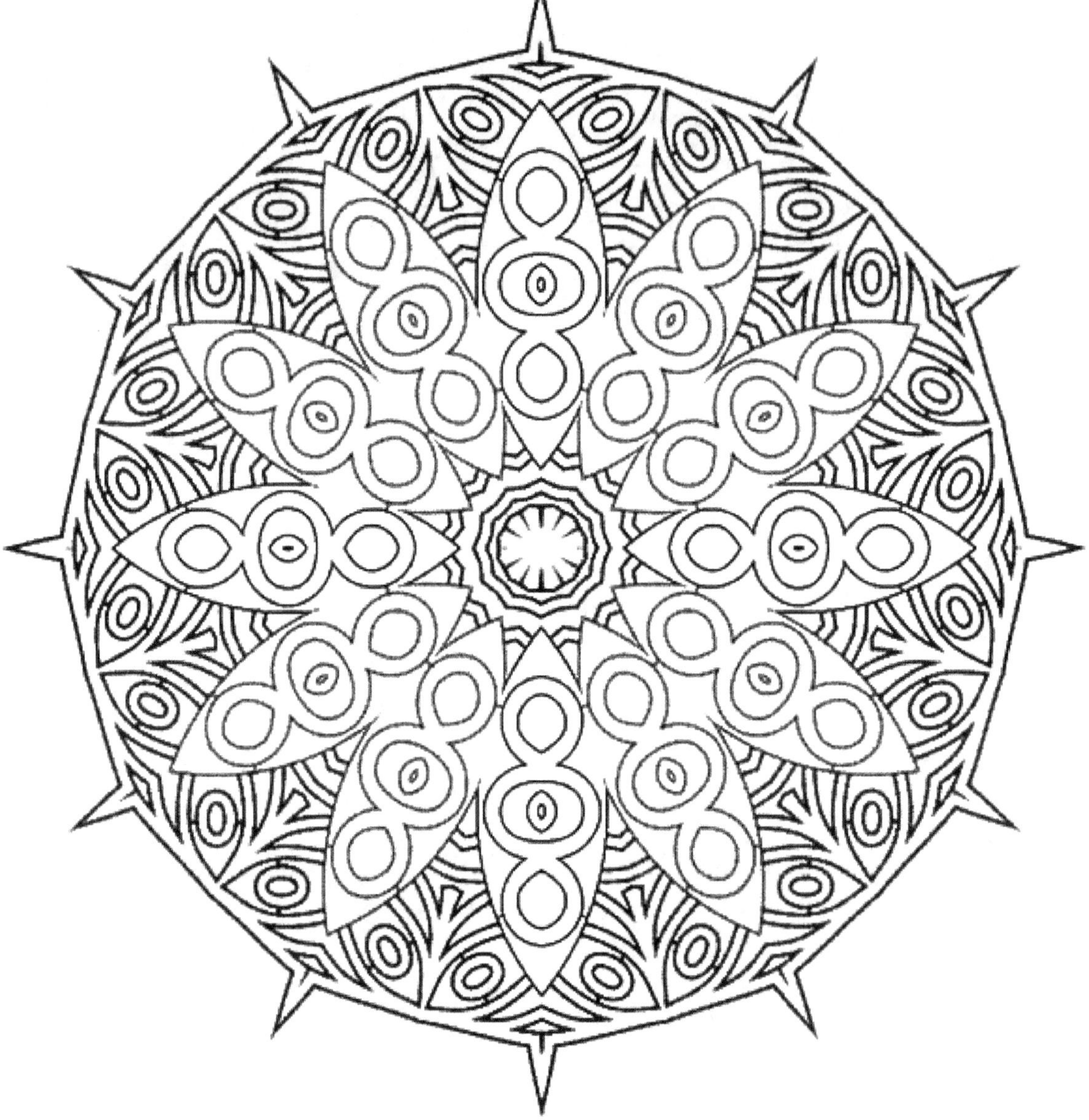

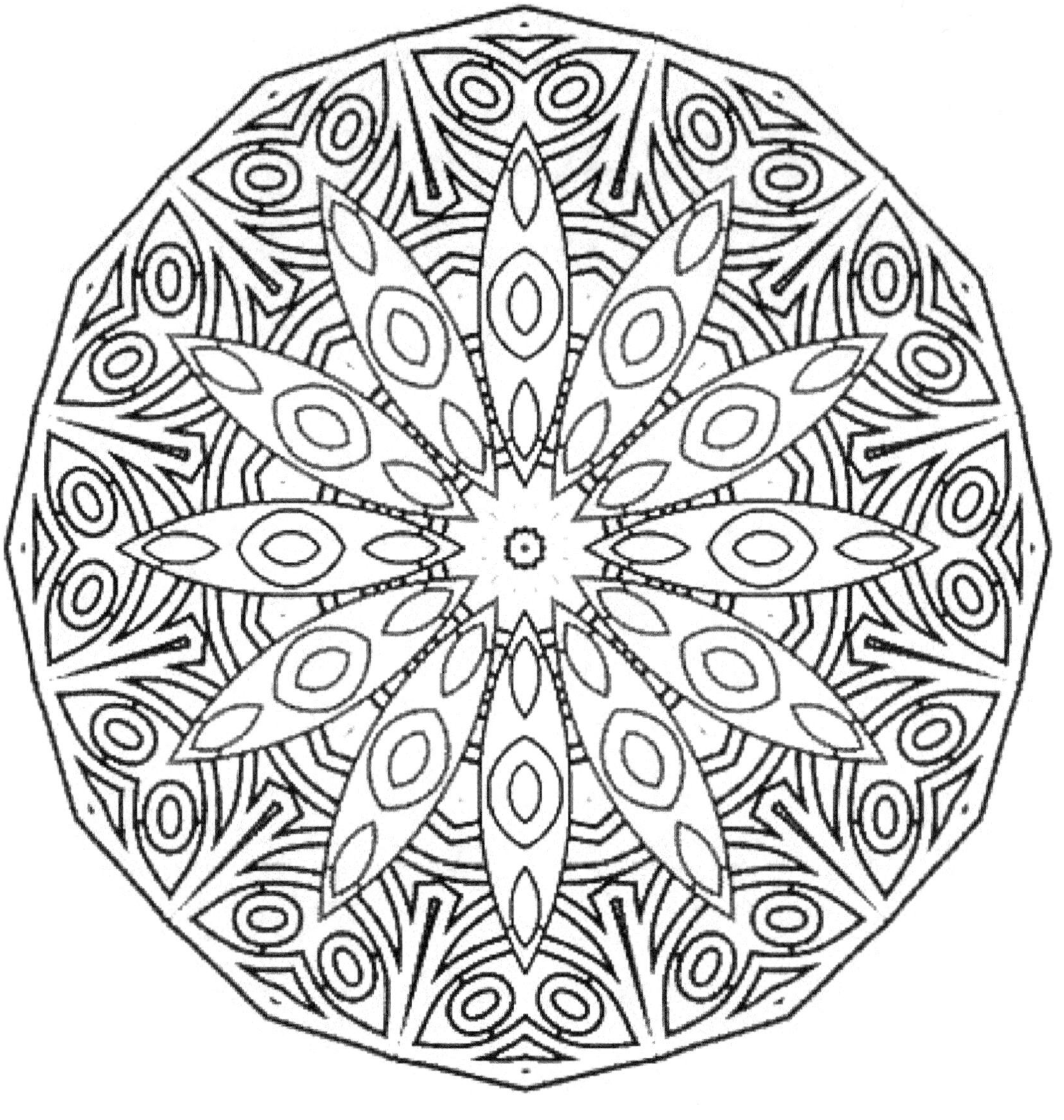

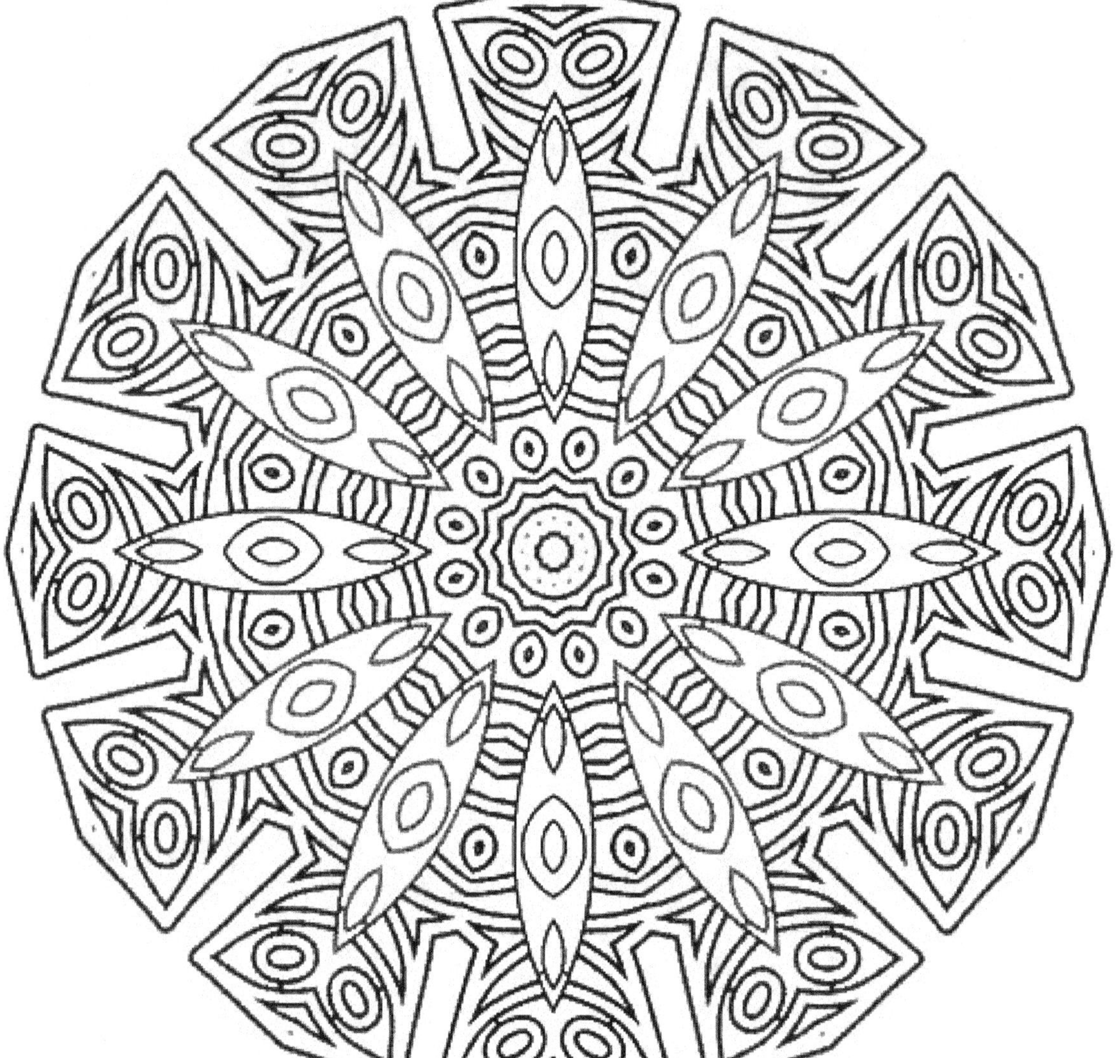

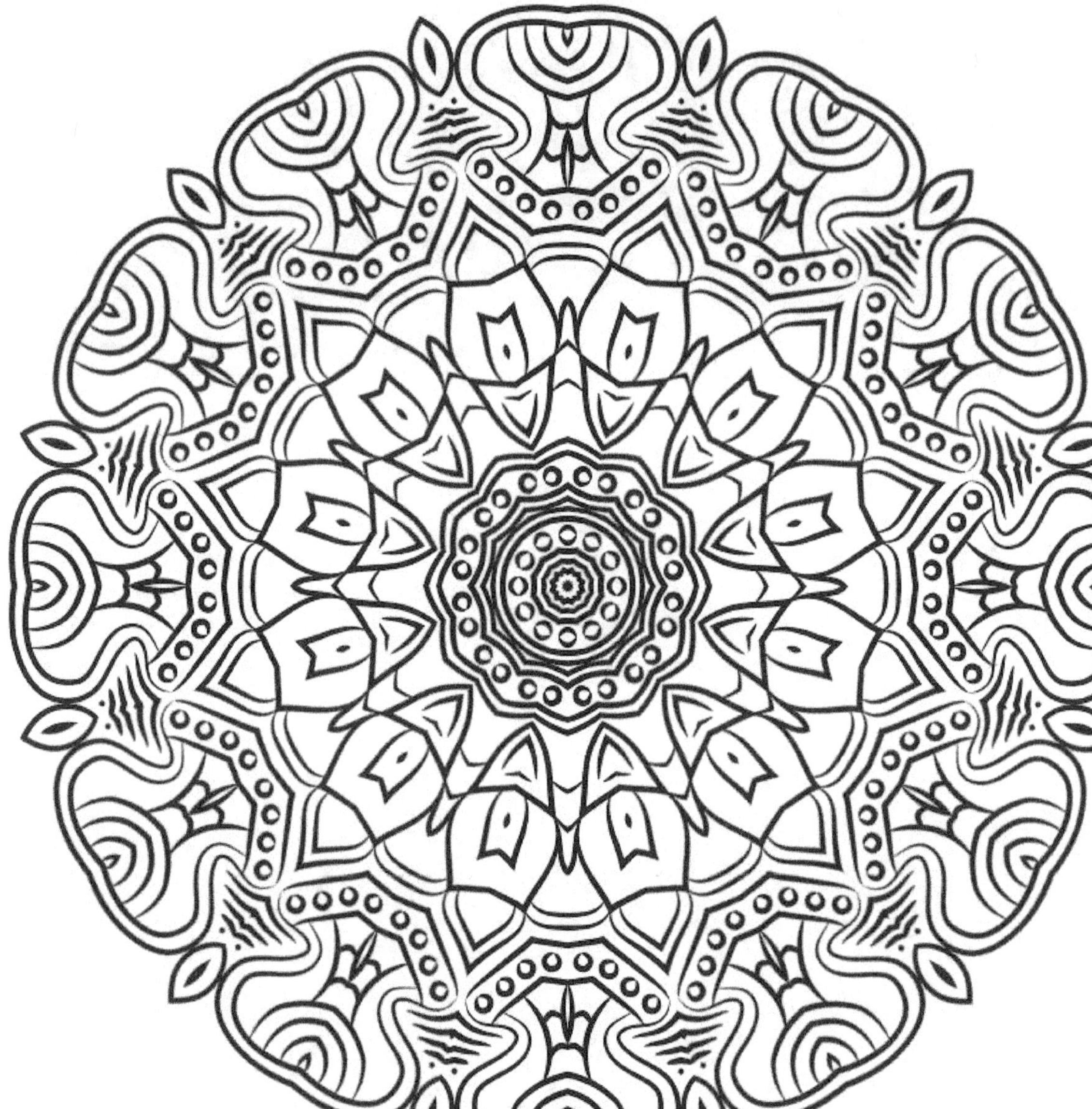

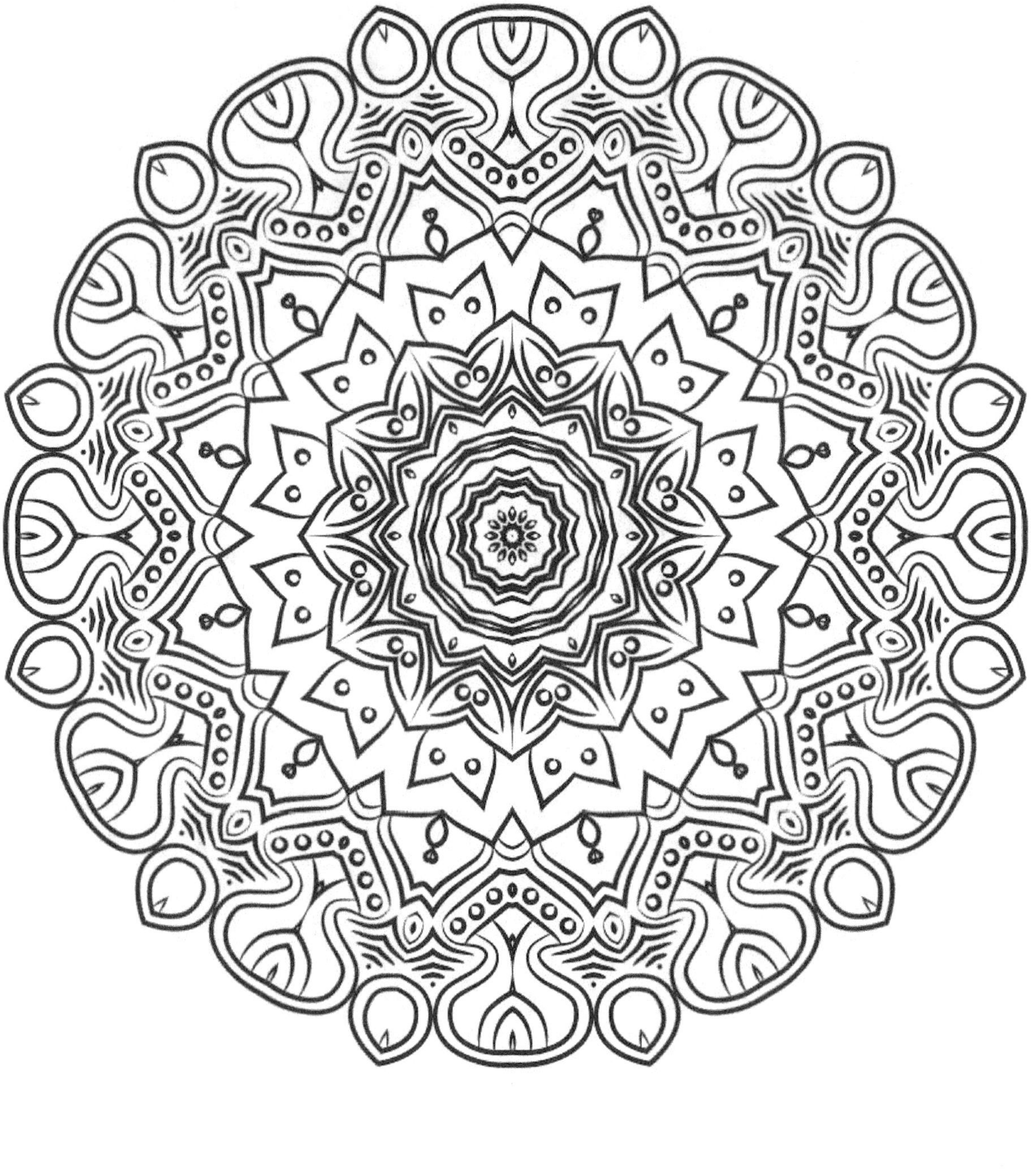

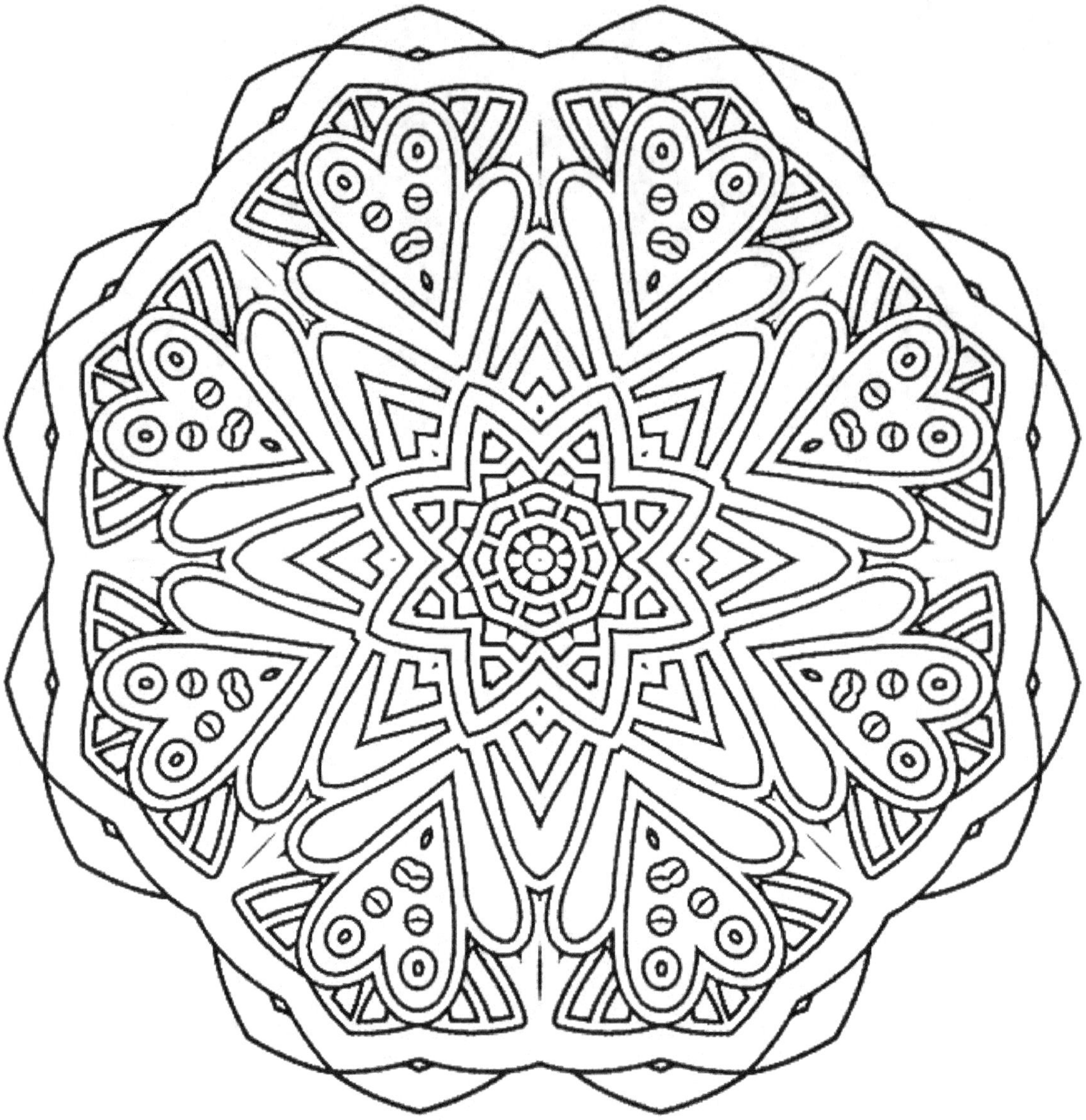

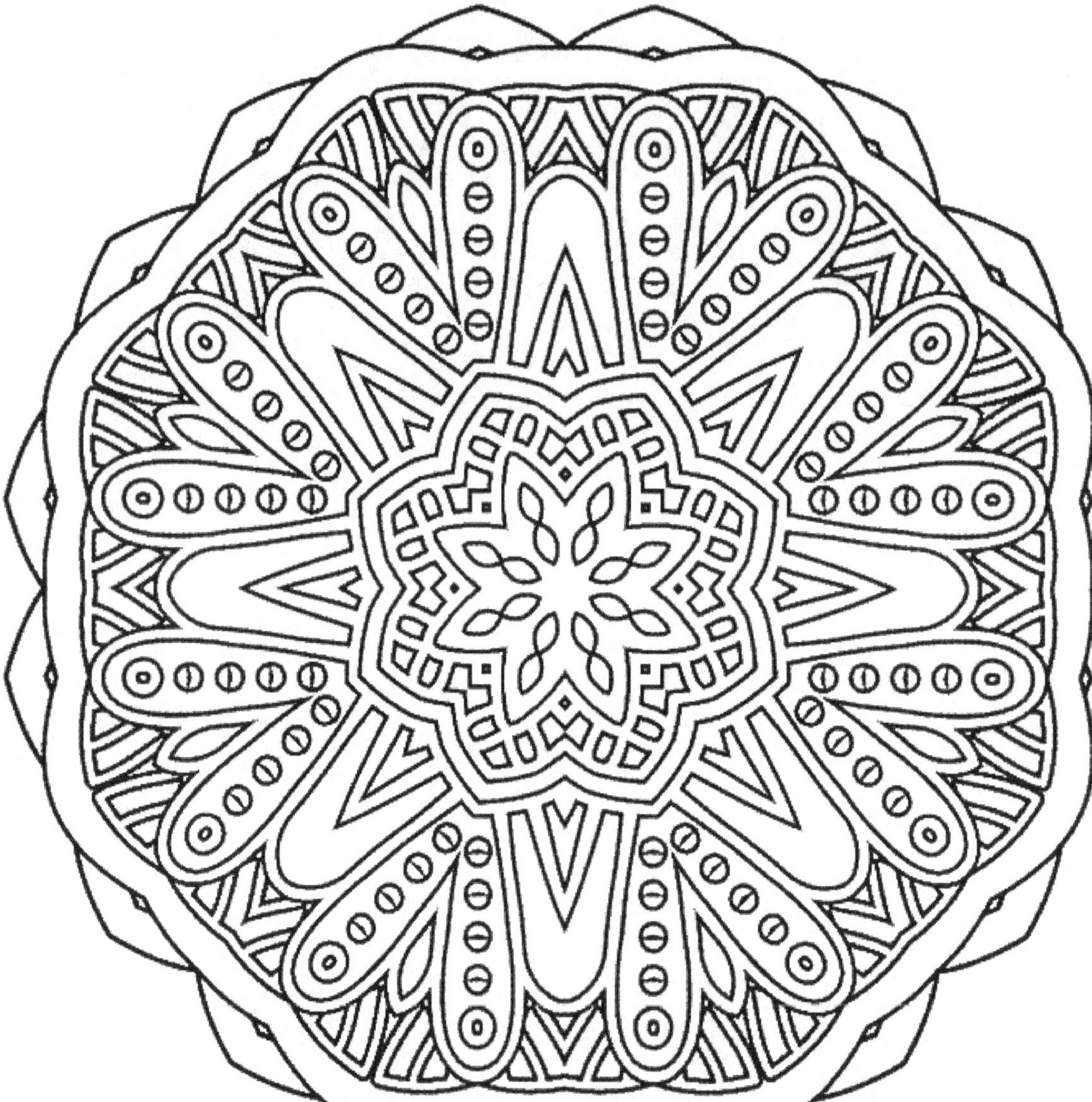

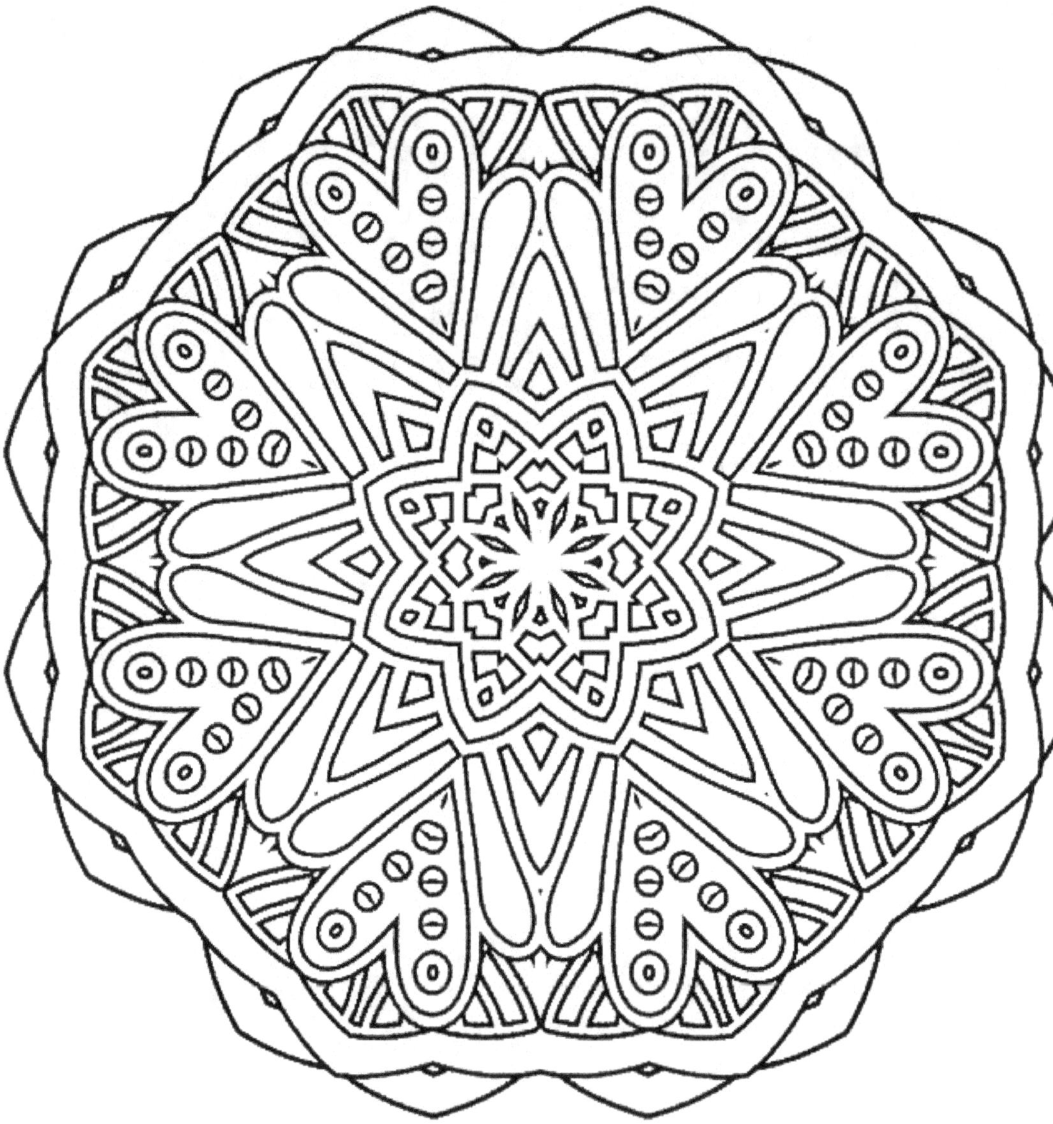

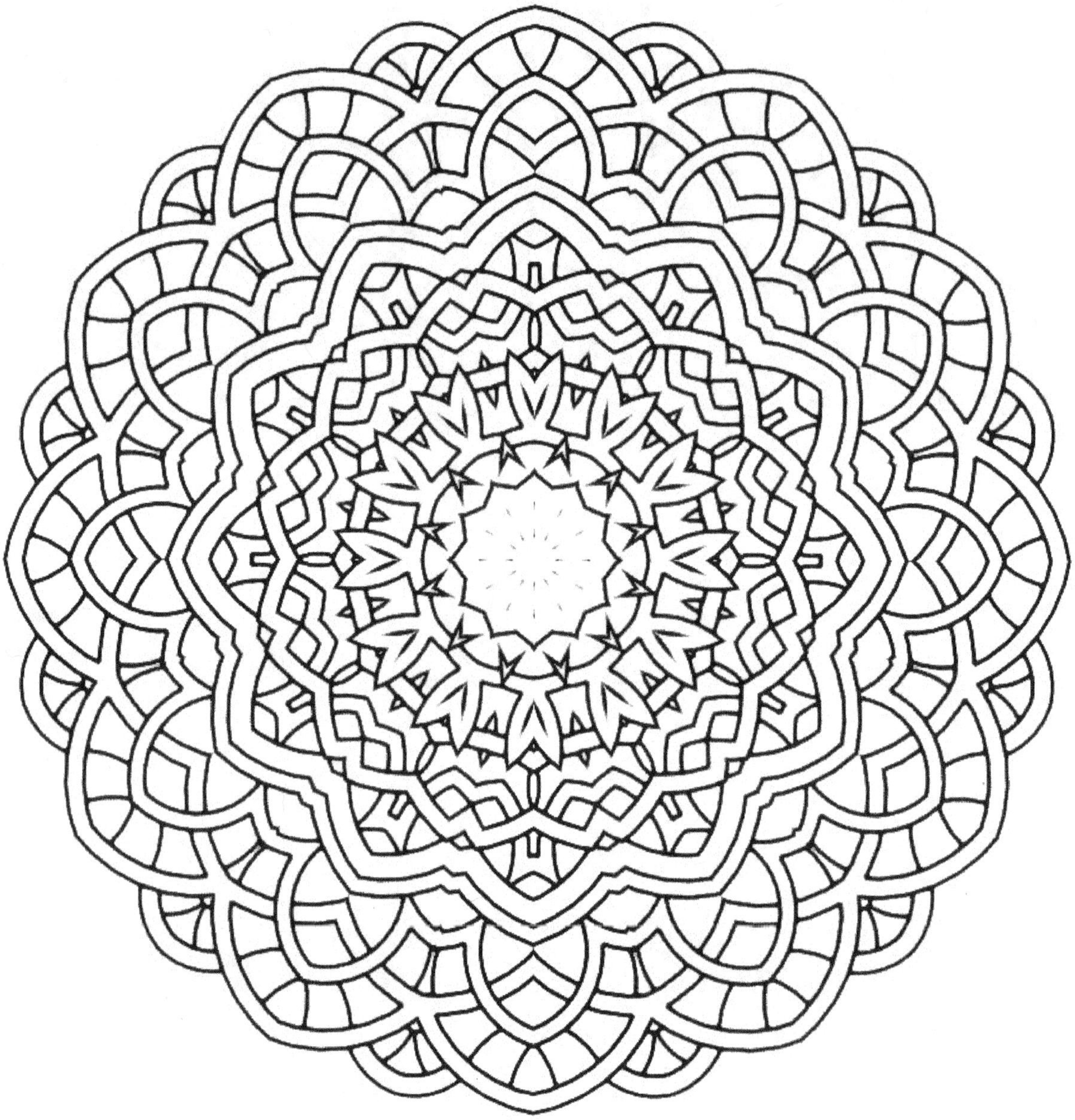

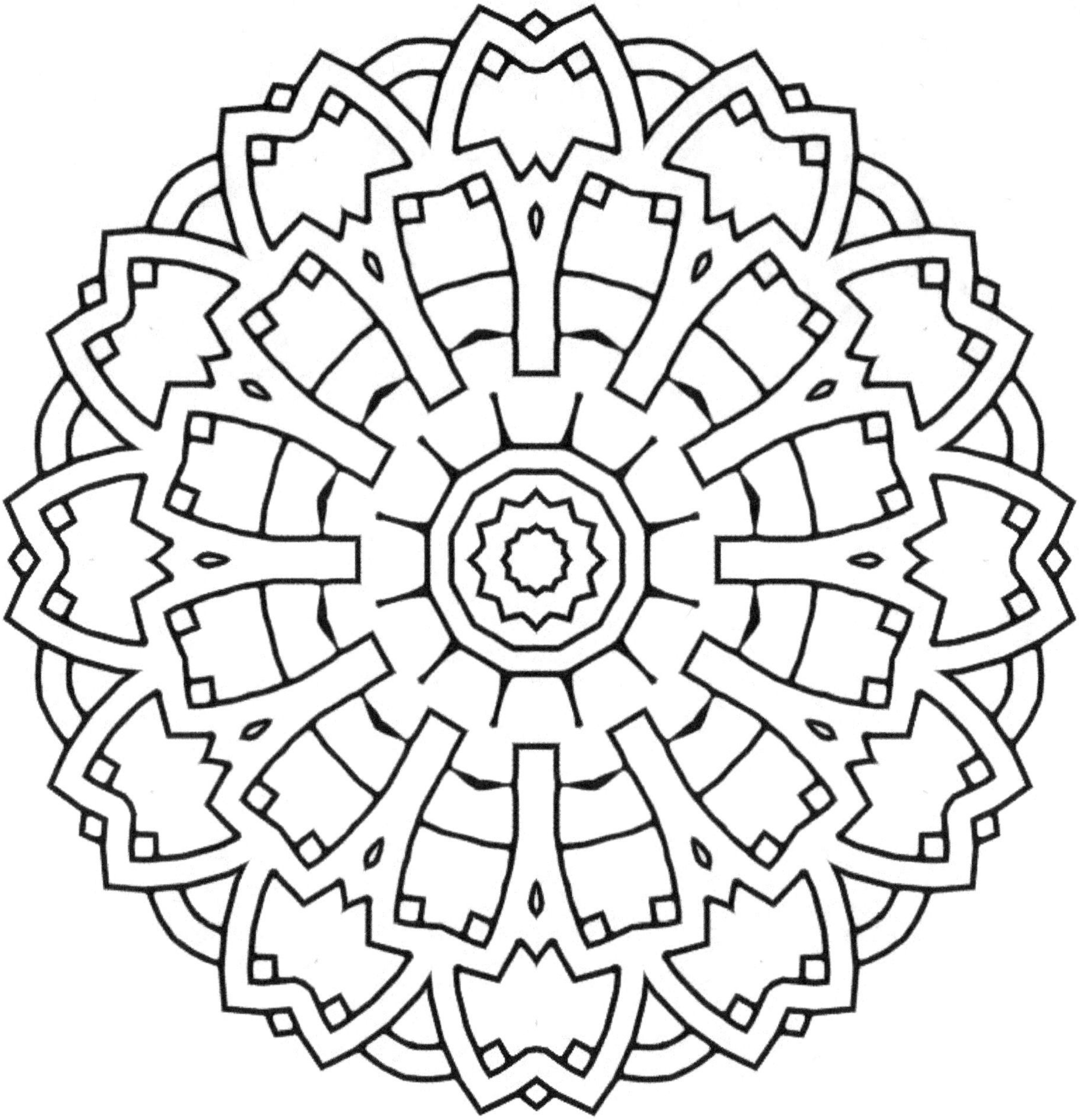

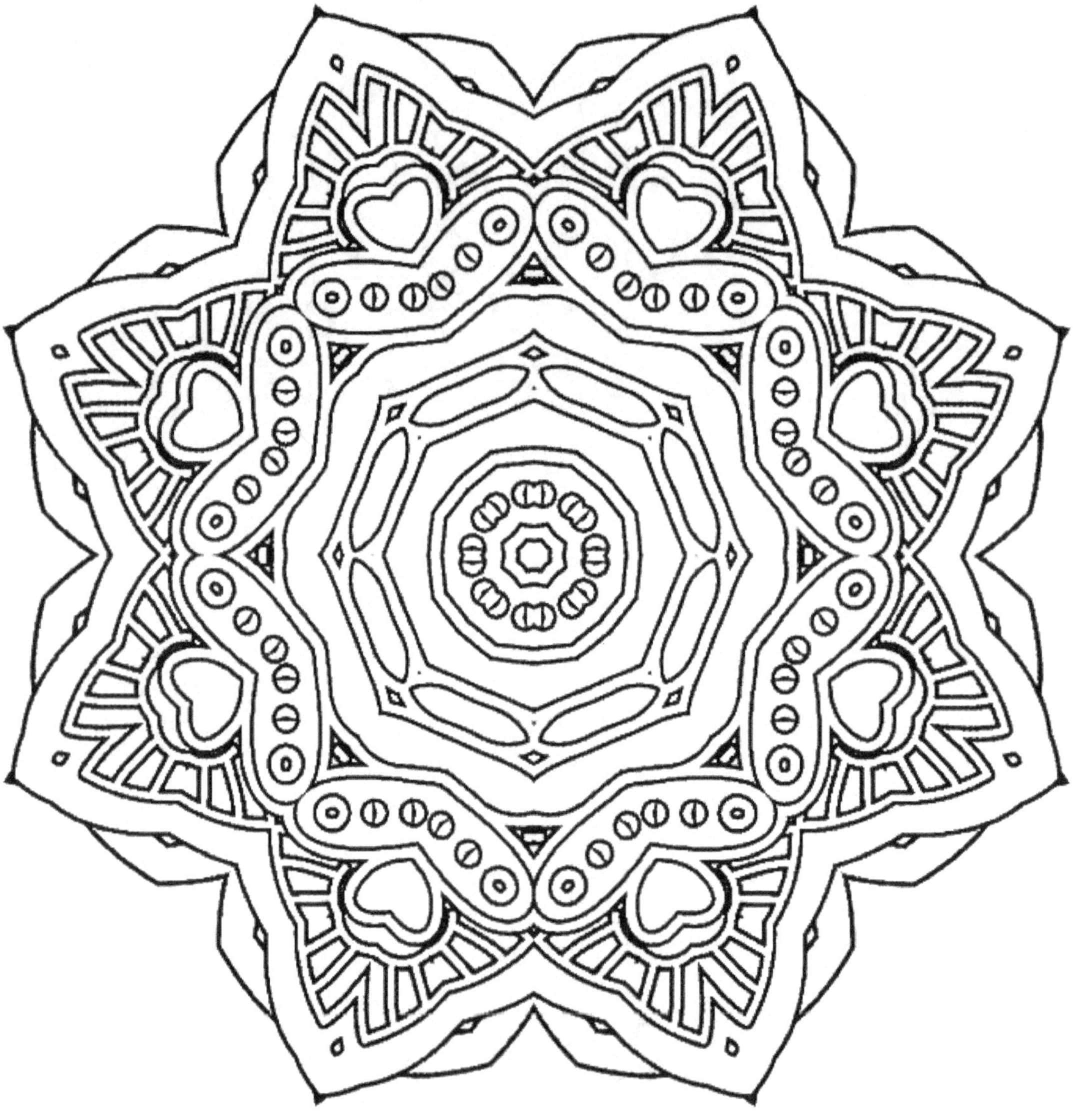

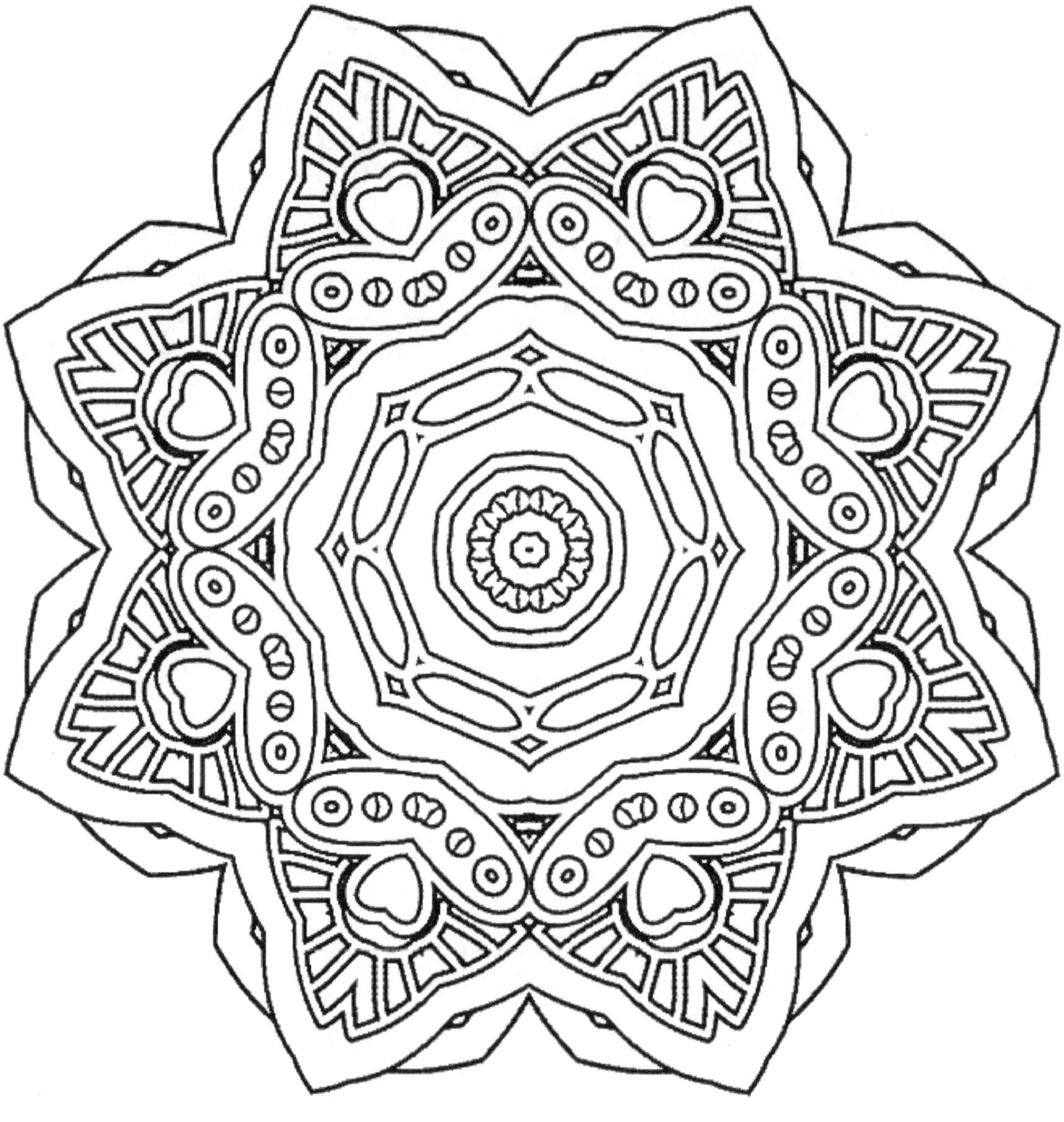

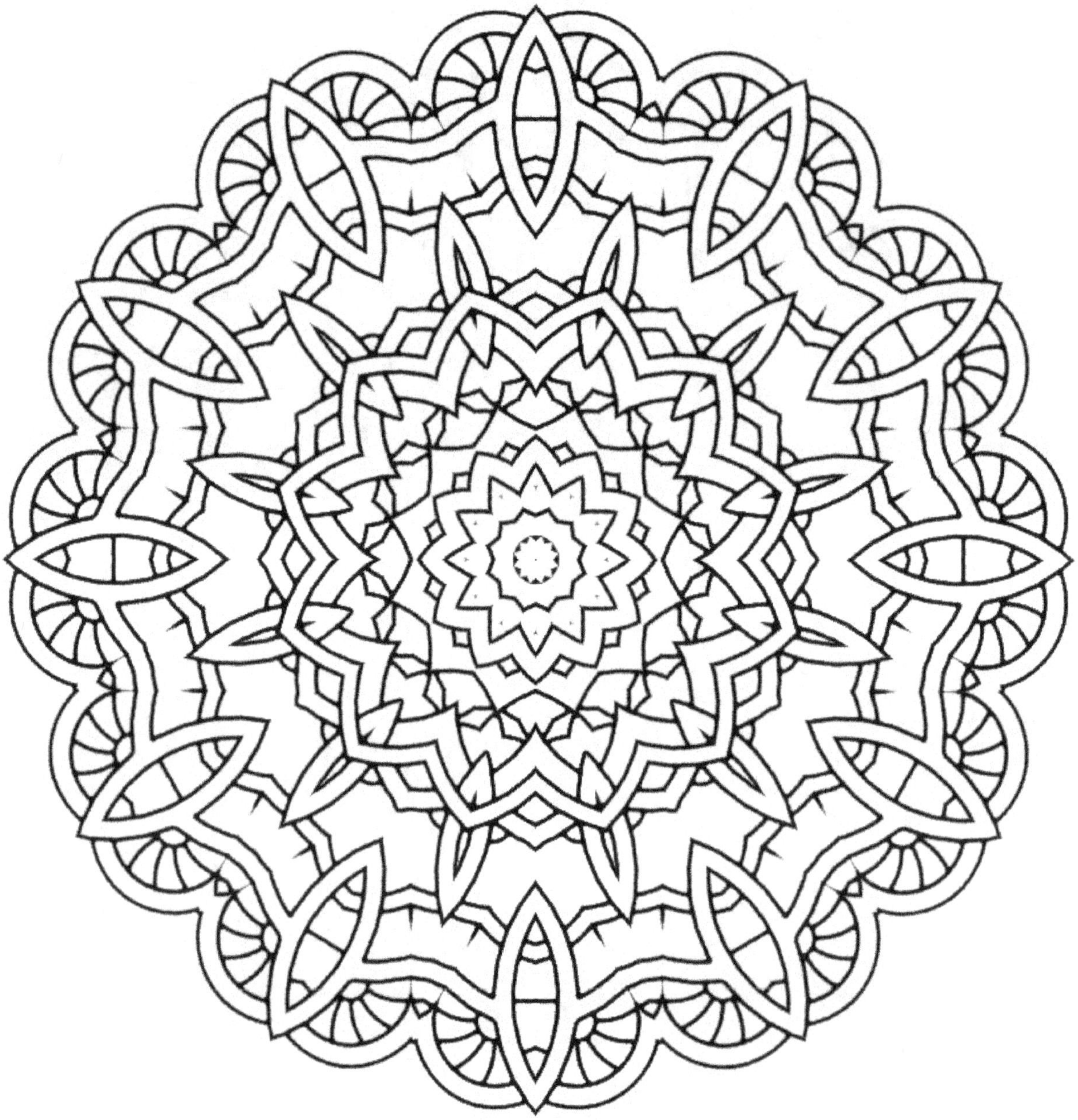

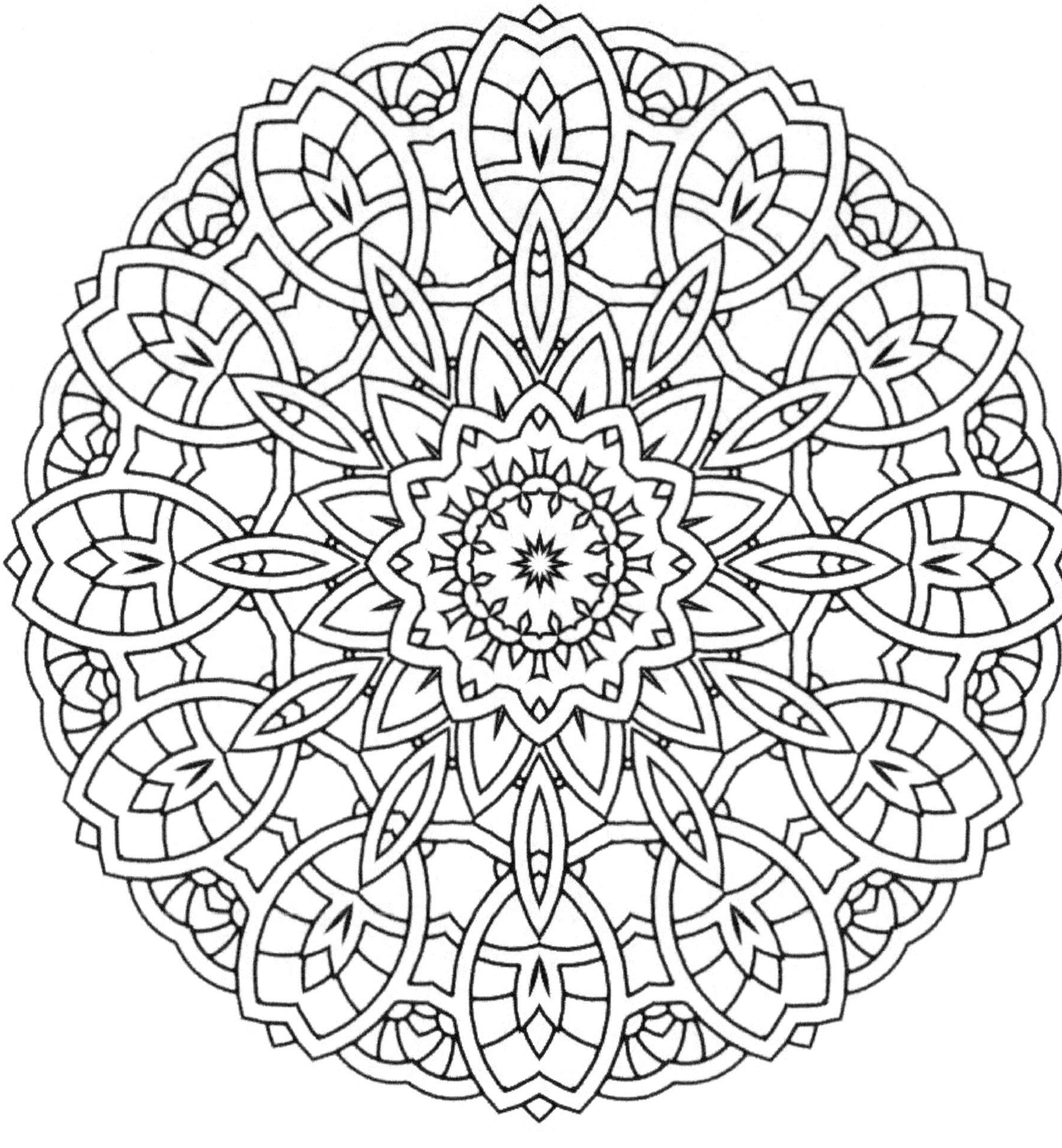

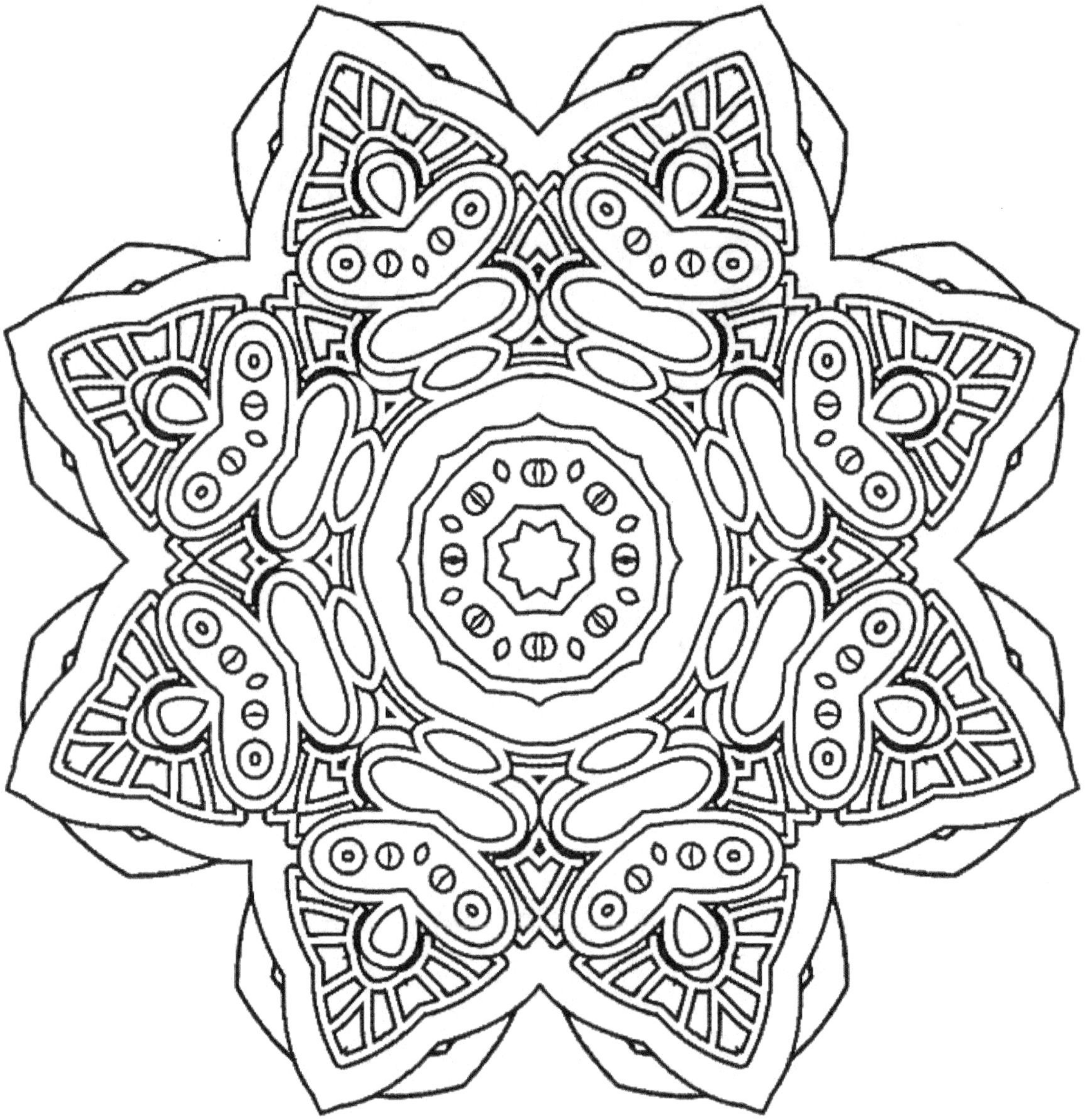

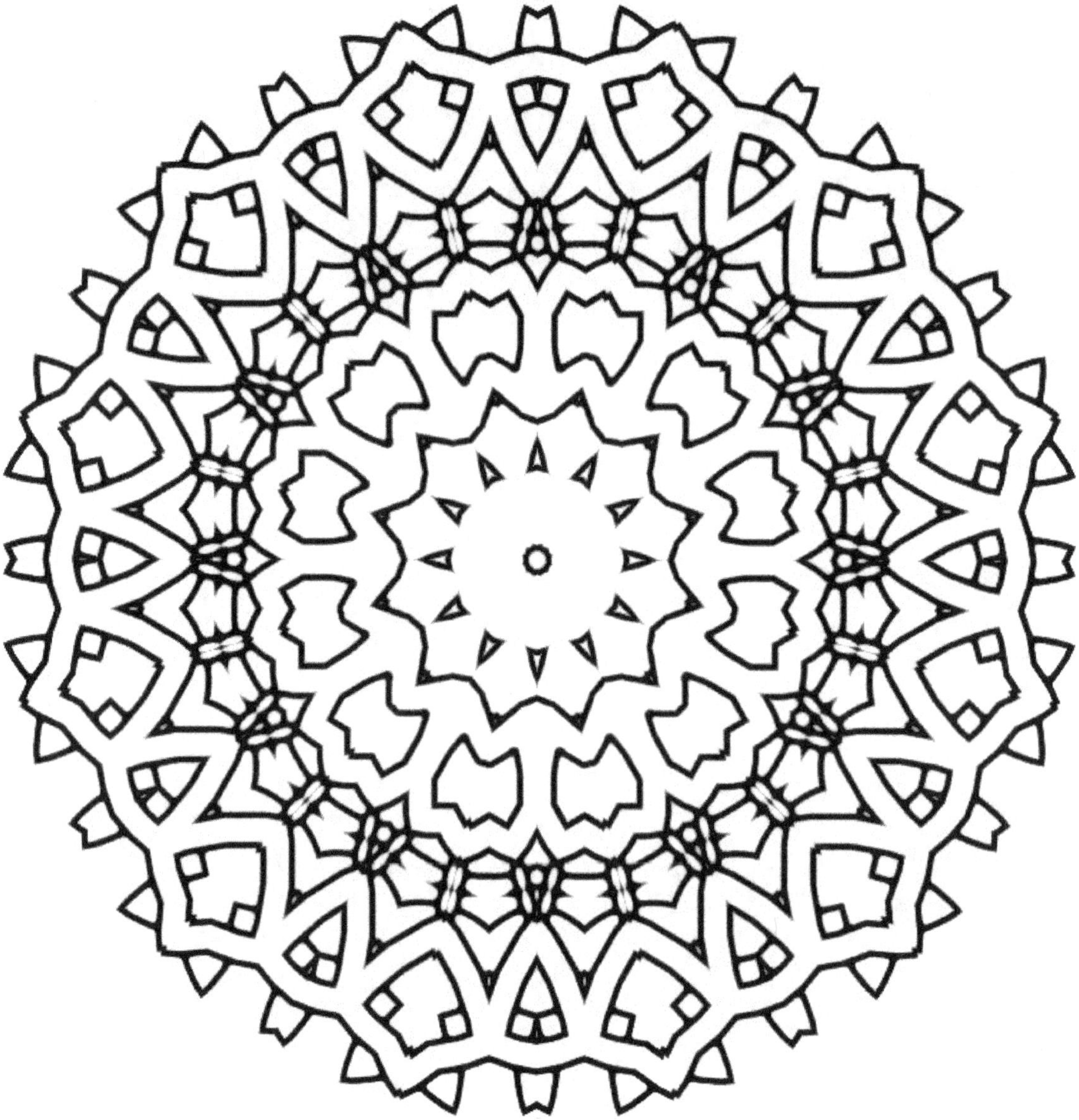

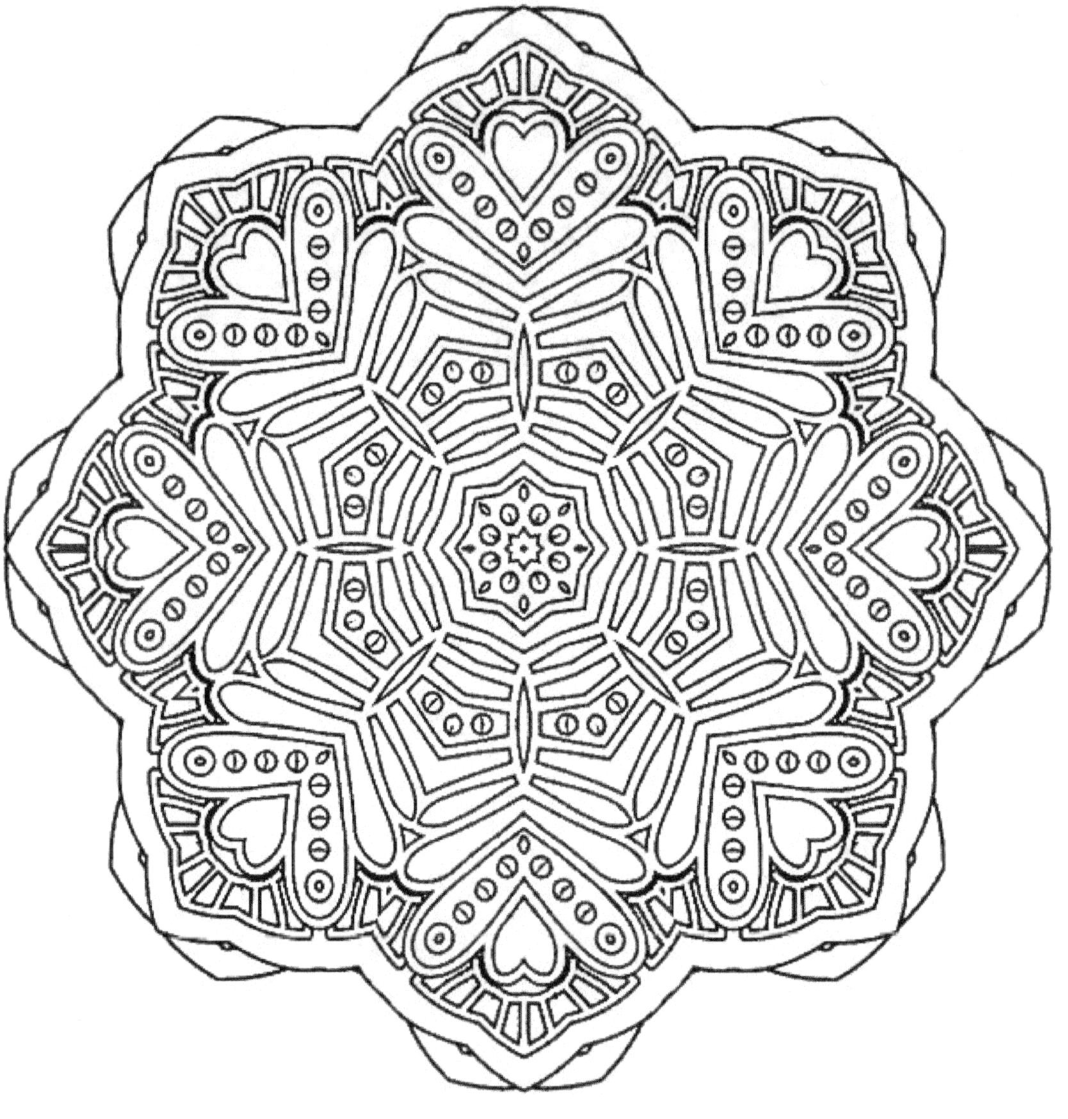

www.ingramcontent.com/pod-product-compliance
Lightning Source LLC
Chambersburg PA
CBHW081128280526
45787CB00007B/3019
9781534849938